WE LOVE BUGS:
31 CLASSIC BUG POEMS FOR KIDS

xist Publishing

About this Collection

For Audrey, my little Entomologist

This collection of poems primarily in the public domain was edited and complied by Calee M. Lee
Oh Roly! My Poly! © 2012 by Calee M. Lee

Contents

Ladybird, Ladybird

Ladybird, ladybird, fly away home,
Your house in on fire and your children are gone,
All except one and her name is Ann,
And she crept under the frying pan.

Fiddle Dee-Dee

Fiddle-dee-dee, fiddle-dee-dee,
The fly has married the bumblebee.
Said the fly, said he,
"Will you marry me,
And live with me sweet bumblebee?"
Fiddle-dee-dee, fiddle-dee-dee,
The fly has married the bumblebee.

LADYBUGS

I saw a little lady bug flying in the air,
But when I tried to catch her, two bugs were there.
Two little lady bugs flew up in a tree.
I tiptoed very quietly, and then I saw three.
Three little lady bugs - I looked for one more.
I saw one sitting on the ground, that made four.
Four little lady bugs - another one arrived.
I saw her sitting on a flower, and that made five.
Five little lady bugs, all red and black -
I clapped my hands and shouted, and they all flew back!

I KNOW A BEETLE

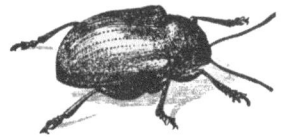

I know a beetle,
Who lives down a drain.
His coat's very shiny,
But terribly plain.
When I take a bath,
He comes up the pipe.
Together we wash,
Together we wipe.

The Ants go Marching

The ants go marching one by one, Hurrah! Hurrah!
The ants go marching one by one,
The little one stops to suck his thumb,
And they all go marching on ...
BOOM! BOOM! BOOM!

The ants go marching two by two, Hurrah! Hurrah!
The ants go marching two by two,
The little one stops to tie his shoe,
And they all go marching on ...
BOOM! BOOM! BOOM!

The ants go marching three by three, Hurrah! Hurrah!
The ants go marching three by three,
The little one stops to climb a tree,
And they all go marching on ...
BOOM! BOOM! BOOM!

The ants go marching four by four, Hurrah! Hurrah!
The ants go marching four by four,
The little one stops to ask for more,
And they all go marching on ...
BOOM! BOOM! BOOM!

The ants go marching five by five, Hurrah! Hurrah!
The ants go marching five by five,
The little one stops to jump and dive,
And they all go marching on ...
BOOM! BOOM! BOOM!

The ants go marching six by six, Hurrah! Hurrah!
The ants go marching six by six,
The little one stops to pick up sticks,
And they all go marching on ...
BOOM! BOOM! BOOM!

The ants go marching seven by seven, Hurrah! Hurrah!
The ants go marching seven by seven,
The little one stops to pray to heaven,
And they all go marching on ...
BOOM! BOOM! BOOM!

The ants go marching eight by eight, Hurrah! Hurrah!
The ants go marching eight by eight,
The little one stops to shut the gate,
And they all go marching on ...
BOOM! BOOM! BOOM!

The ants go marching nine by nine, Hurrah! Hurrah!
The ants go marching nine by nine,
The little one stops to check the time,
And they all go marching on ...
BOOM! BOOM! BOOM!

The ants go marching ten by ten,
Hurrah! Hurrah!
The ants go marching ten by ten,
But the little one stops to say ...
"THE END"!

Little Miss Muffet

Little Miss Muffet sat on a tuffet,
Eating her curds and whey.
There came a big spider,
Who sat down beside her.
And frightened Miss Muffet away!

Itsy Bitsy Spider

The Itsy Bitsy spider went up the water spout
Down came the rain and washed the spider out.
Out came the sun and dried up all the rain,
Now Itsy Bitsy spider went up the spout again!

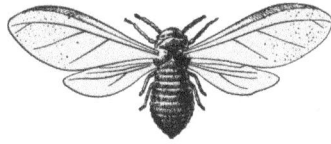

BEES

A swarm of bees in May,
Is worth a load of hay.
A swarm of bees in June,
Is worth a silver spoon.
A swarm of bees in July,
Isn't worth a fly.
A Flea and a Fly
A flea and a fly
Flew up in a flue.
Said the flea, "Let us fly!"
Said the fly, "Let us flee!"
So they flew through a flap in the flue.

There was an Old Lady

There was an old lady who swallowed a fly,
I don't know why she swallowed a fly.
Perhaps she'll die!

There was an old lady who swallowed a spider,
That wriggled and jiggled and tickled inside her.
She swallowed the spider to catch the fly,
I don't know why she swallowed a fly.
Perhaps she'll die!

There was an old lady who swallowed a bird,
How absurd to swallow a bird.
She swallowed the bird to catch the spider,
She swallowed the spider to catch the fly,
I don't know why she swallowed a fly.
Perhaps she'll die!

There was an old lady who swallowed a cat,
Imagine that, she swallowed a cat.
She swallowed the cat to catch the bird,
She swallowed the bird to catch the spider,
She swallowed the spider to catch the fly,
I don't know why she swallowed a fly.
Perhaps she'll die!

There was an old lady who swallowed a dog,
Oh, what a hog to swallow a dog.
She swallowed the dog to catch the cat,
She swallowed the cat to catch the bird,
She swallowed the bird to catch the spider,
She swallowed the spider to catch the fly,
I don't know why she swallowed a fly.
Perhaps she'll die!

There was an old lady who swallowed a goat,
She just opened her throat and swallowed a goat!
She swallowed the goat to catch the dog,
She swallowed the dog to catch the cat,
She swallowed the cat to catch the bird,
She swallowed the bird to catch the spider,
She swallowed the spider to catch the fly,
I don't know why she swallowed a fly.
Perhaps she'll die!

There was an old lady who swallowed a cow,
I'm not sure how she swallowed a cow.
She swallowed the cow to catch the goat,
She swallowed the goat to catch the dog,
She swallowed the dog to catch the cat,
She swallowed the cat to catch the bird,
She swallowed the bird to catch the spider,
She swallowed the spider to catch the fly,
I don't know why she swallowed a fly.
Perhaps she'll die!

There was an old lady who swallowed a horse.
She's dead, of course!

The Spider

By Jane Taylor

"Oh, look at that great ugly spider!" said Ann;
And screaming, she brush'd it away with her fan;
"Tis a frightful black creature as ever can be,
I wish that it would not come crawling on me."
"Indeed," said her mother, "I'll venture to say,
The poor thing will try to keep out of your way;
For after the fright, and the fall, and the pain,
It has much more occasion than you to complain.
"But why should you dread the poor insect, my dear?
If it hurt you, there'd be some excuse for your fear;
But its little black legs, as it hurried away,
Did but tickle your arm, as they went, I dare say.
"For them to fear us we must grant to be just,
Who in less than a moment can tread them to dust;
But certainly we have no cause for alarm;
For, were they to try, they could do us no harm.
"Now look! it has got to its home; do you see
What a delicate web it has spun in the tree?
Why here, my dear Ann, is a lesson for you:
Come learn from this spider what patience can do!
"And when at your business you're tempted to play,
Recollect what you see in this insect to-day,
Or else, to your shame, it may seem to be true,
That a poor little spider is wiser than you."

The bee is not afraid of me

The bee is not afraid of me,
I know the butterfly;
The pretty people in the woods
Receive me cordially.

The brooks laugh louder when I come,
The breezes madder play.
Wherefore, mine eyes, thy silver mists?
Wherefore, O summer's day?

from Nonsense Alphabet

BY Edward Lear

A
A was an ant
Who seldom stood still,
And who made a nice house
In the side of a hill.
a
Nice little ant!

The Cricket Sang

By Emily Dickinson

The cricket sang,
And set the sun,
And workmen finished, one by one,
Their seam the day upon.
The low grass loaded with the dew,
The twilight stood as strangers do
With hat in hand, polite and new,
To stay as if, or go.
A vastness, as a neighbor, came,--
A wisdom without face or name,
A peace, as hemispheres at home,--
And so the night became.

Baby Bye

By Theodore Tilon

Baby bye
Here's a fly,
Let us watch him, you and I,
How he crawls
Up the walls
Yet he never falls.

Old Man and a Bee

By Theodore Tilton

There was an old man in a tree
Who was horribly bored by a bee;
When they said, "Does it buzz?"
He replied. "Yes, it does!
It's a regular brute of a bee!"

Caterpillar

By Christina Rossetti

Brown and furry
Caterpillar in a hurry,
Take your walk
To the shady leaf, or stalk,
Or what not,
Which may be the chosen spot.
No toad spy you,
Hovering bird of prey pass by you;
Spin and die,
To live again a butterfly.

On the Grasshopper and the Cricket

By John Keats

The poetry of earth is never dead:
When all the birds are faint with the hot sun,
And hide in cooling trees, a voice will run
From hedge to hedge about the new-mown mead;
That is the Grasshopper's -- he takes the lead
In summer luxury, -- he has never done
With his delights; for when tired out with fun
He rests at ease beneath some pleasant weed.
The poetry of earth is ceasing never:
On a lone winter evening, when the frost
Has wrought a silence, from the stove there shrills
The Cricket's song, in warmth increasing ever,
And seems to one in drowsiness half lost,
The Grasshopper's among some grassy hills.

The Fly

By William Blake

Little Fly,
Thy summer's play
My thoughtless hand
Has brushed away.

Am not I
A fly like thee?
Or art not thou
A man like me?

For I dance
And drink, and sing,
Till some blind hand
Shall brush my wing.

If thought is life
And strength and breath,
And the want
Of thought is death;

Then am I
A happy fly,
If I live,
Or if I die.

Butterfly Laughter

By Katherine Mansfield

In the middle of our porridge plates
There was a blue butterfly painted
And each morning we tried who should reach the butterfly first.
Then the Grandmother said: "Do not eat the poor butterfly."
That made us laugh.
Always she said it and always it started us laughing.
It seemed such a sweet little joke.
I was certain that one fine morning
The butterfly would fly out of our plates,
Laughing the teeniest laugh in the world,
And perch on the Grandmother's lap.

Blue Butterfly Day

By Robert Frost

It is blue-butterfly day here in spring,
And with these sky-flakes down in flurry on flurry
There is more unmixed color on the wing
Than flowers will show for days unless they hurry.

But these are flowers that fly and all but sing:
And now from having ridden out desire
They lie closed over in the wind and cling
Where wheels have freshly sliced the April mire.

How soft a Caterpillar steps

By Emily Dickinson

How soft a Caterpillar steps—
I fond one on my Hand
From such a velvet world it comes
Such plushes at command
Its soundless travels just arrest
My slow—terrestrial eye
Intent upon its own career
What use has it for me—

CLOCK-A-CLAY

(A LADYBUG)

By Emily Dickinson

In the cowslip pips I lie,
Hidden from the buzzing fly,
While green grass beneath me lies,
Pearled with dew like fishes' eyes,
Here I lie, a clock-a-clay,
Waiting for the time of day.
While the forest quakes surprise,
And the wild wind sobs and sighs,
My home rocks as like to fall,
On its pillar green and tall;
When the pattering rain drives by
Clock-a-clay keeps warm and dry.
Day by day and night by night,
All the week I hide from sight;
In the cowslip pips I lie,
In rain and dew still warm and dry;
Day and night, and night and day,
Red, black-spotted clock-a-clay.
My home shakes in wind and showers,
Pale green pillar topped with flowers,
Bending at the wild wind's breath,
Till I touch the grass beneath;
Here I live, lone clock-a-clay,
Watching for the time of day.

Verses on a Butterfly

By Joseph Warton

Fair Child of Sun and Summer! we behold
With eager eyes thy wings bedropp'd with gold;
The purple spots that o'er thy mantle spread,
The sapphire's lively blue, the ruby's red,
Ten thousand various blended tints surprise,
Beyond the rainbow's hues or peacock's eyes:
Not Judah's king in eastern pomp array'd,
Whose charms allur'd from far the Sheban maid,
High on his glitt'ring throne, like you could shine
(Nature's completest miniature divine):
For thee the rose her balmy buds renews,
And silver lilies fill their cups with dews;
Flora for thee the laughing fields perfumes,
For thee Pomona sheds her choicest blooms,
Soft Zephyr wafts thee on his gentlest gales
O'er Hackwood's sunny hill and verdant vales;
For thee, gay queen of insects! do we rove
From walk to walk, from beauteous grove to grove;
And let the critics know, whose pedant pride
And awkward jests our sprightly sport deride:
That all who honours, fame, or wealth pursue,
Change but the name of things--they hunt for you.

To A Butterfly

(first poem)

By William Wordsworth

Stay near me - do not take thy flight!
A little longer stay in sight!
Much converse do I find in thee,
Historian of my infancy!
Float near me; do not yet depart! Dead times revive in thee:
Thou bring'st, gay creature as thou art!
A solemn image to my heart,
My father's family!
Oh! pleasant, pleasant were the days,
The time, when, in our childish plays,
My sister Emmeline and I
Together chased the butterfly!
A very hunter did I rush
Upon the prey: - with leaps and springs
I followed on from brake to bush;
But she, God love her, feared to brush
The dust from off its wings.

To A Butterfly

(second poem)

By William Wordsworth

I've watched you now a full half-hour,
Self-poised upon that yellow flower;
And, little Butterfly! indeed
I know not if you sleep or feed.
How motionless!---not frozen seas
More motionless! and then
What joy awaits you, when the breeze
Hath found you out among the trees,
And calls you forth again !
This plot of orchard-ground is ours;
My trees they are, my Sister's flowers;
Here rest your wing when they are weary;
Here lodge as in a sanctuary!
Come often to us, fear no wrong;
Sit near us on the bough!
We'll talk of sunshine and of song,
And summer days, when we were young;
Sweet childish days, that were as long
As twenty days are now.

The Bee and the Butterfly

By Mary Darby Robinson

UPON a garden's perfum'd bed
With various gaudy colours spread,
Beneath the shelter of a ROSE
A BUTTERFLY had sought repose;
Faint, with the sultry beams of day,
Supine the beauteous insect lay.
A BEE, impatient to devour
The nectar sweets of ev'ry flow'r,
Returning to her golden store,
A weight of fragrant treasure bore;
With envious eye, she mark'd the shade,
Where the poor BUTTERFLY was laid,
And resting on the bending spray,
Thus murmur'd forth her drony lay:
"Thou empty thing, whose merit lies
In the vain boast of orient dies;
Whose glittering form the slightest breath
Robs of its gloss, and fades to death;
Who idly rov'st the summer day,
Flutt'ring a transient life away,
Unmindful of the chilling hour,
The nipping frost, the drenching show'r;
Who heedless of "to-morrow's fare,"
Mak'st present bliss thy only care;
Is it for THEE, the damask ROSE
With such transcendent lustre glows?

Is it for such a giddy thing
Nature unveils the blushing spring?
Hence, from thy lurking place, and know,
'Tis not for THEE her beauties glow."
The BUTTERFLY, with decent pride,
In gentle accents, thus reply'd:
"'Tis true, I flutter life away
In pastime, innocent and gay;
The SUN that decks the blushing spring
Gives lustre to my painted wing;
'Tis NATURE bids each colour vie,
With rainbow tints of varying die;
I boast no skill, no subtle pow'r
To steal the balm from ev'ry flow'r;
The ROSE, that only shelter'd ME,
Has pour'd a load of sweets on THEE;
Of merit we have both our share,
Heav'n gave thee ART, and made me FAIR;

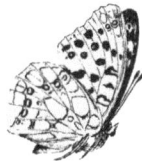

The Dragon-fly

By Walter Savage Landor

Life (priest and poet say) is but a dream;
I wish no happier one than to be laid
Beneath a cool syringa's scented shade,
Or wavy willow, by the running stream,
Brimful of moral, where the dragon-fly,
Wanders as careless and content as I.
Thanks for this fancy, insect king,
Of purple crest and filmy wing,
Who with indifference givest up
The water-lily's golden cup,
To come again and overlook
What I am writing in my book.
Believe me, most who read the line
Will read with hornier eyes than thine;
And yet their souls shall live for ever,
And thine drop dead into the river!
God pardon them, O insect king,
Who fancy so unjust a thing!

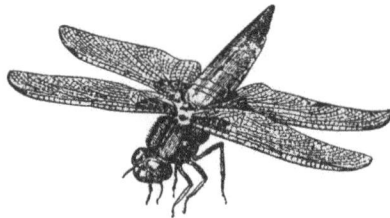

The Glow-worm

By William Wordsworth

Among all lovely things my Love had been;
Had noticed well the stars, all flowers that grew
About her home; but she had never seen
A Glow-worm, never one, and this I knew.
While riding near her home one stormy night
A single glow-worm did I chance to espy;
I gave a fervent welcome to the sight,
And from my horse I leapt; great joy had I.
Upon a leaf the glow-worm did I lay,
To bear it with me through the stormy night:
And, as before, it shone without dismay;
Albeit putting forth a fainter light.
When to the dwelling of my Love I came,
I went into the orchard quietly;
And left the glow-worm, blessing it by name,
Laid safely by itself, beneath a tree.
The whole next day, I hoped, and hoped with fear;
At night the glow-worm shone beneath the tree;
I led my Lucy to the spot, 'Look here,'
Oh! joy it was for her, and joy for me!

The Spider and the Fly

By Mary Howitt

Will you walk into my parlour?"
said the Spider to the Fly,
'Tis the prettiest little parlour that ever you did spy;
The way into my parlour is up a winding stair,
And I've a many curious things to show
when you are there."
Oh no, no," said the little Fly, "to ask me is in vain,
For who goes up your winding stair can
ne'er come down again."
"I'm sure you must be weary, dear,
with soaring up so high;
Will you rest upon my little bed?"
said the Spider to the Fly.
"There are pretty curtains drawn around;
the sheets are fine and thin,
And if you like to rest awhile,
I'll snugly tuck you in!"
Oh no, no," said the little Fly,
"for I've often heard it said,
They never, never wake again,
who sleep upon your bed!"
Said the cunning Spider to the Fly,
" Dear friend what can I do,
To prove the warm affection I 've always
felt for you?
I have within my pantry, good store of
all that's nice;
I'm sure you're very welcome --

will you please to take a slice?"
"Oh no, no," said the little Fly,
"kind Sir, that cannot be,
I've heard what's in your pantry,
and I do not wish to see!" "Sweet creature!"
said the Spider,
"you're witty and you're wise,
How handsome are your gauzy wings,
how brilliant are your eyes!
I've a little looking-glass upon my parlour shelf,
If you'll step in one moment, dear,
you shall behold yourself."
"I thank you, gentle sir," she said,
"for what you 're pleased to say,
And bidding you good morning now,
I'll call another day."
The Spider turned him round about,
and went into his den,
For well he knew the silly Fly would soon
come back again:
So he wove a subtle web, in a little corner sly,
And set his table ready, to dine upon the Fly.
Then he came out to his door again,
and merrily did sing,
"Come hither, hither, pretty Fly,
with the pearl and silver wing;
Your robes are green and purple --
there's a crest upon your head;
Your eyes are like the diamond bright,
but mine are dull as lead!"
Alas, alas! how very soon this silly little Fly,
Hearing his wily, flattering words,
came slowly flitting by;
With buzzing wings she hung aloft,

then near and nearer drew,
Thinking only of her brilliant eyes,
and green and purple hue --
Thinking only of her crested head --
poor foolish thing! At last,
Up jumped the cunning Spider,
and fiercely held her fast.
He dragged her up his winding stair,
into his dismal den,
Within his little parlour --
but she ne'er came out again!
An now dear little children,
who may this story read,
To idle, silly flattering words,
I pray you ne'er give heed:
Unto an evil counselor,
close heart and ear and eye,
And take a lesson from this tale,
of the Spider and the Fly.

Oh Roly! My Poly!

By Calee M. Lee

Oh Roly! my Poly! Curled up in your ball,
Why are you hiding in a crescent so small?
My fingers are gentle, your body won't squish.
Oh Roly! My Poly! For your tickles I wish.

THE FLEA

By John Donne

Cruel and sudden, hast thou since
Purpled thy nail in blood of innocence?
Wherein could this flea guilty be,
Except in that drop which it sucked from thee?
Yet thou triumph'st and say'st that thou
Find'st not thyself, nor me the weaker now;
'Tis true, then learn how false fears be:
Just so much honor, when thou yield'st to me,
Will waste, as this flea's death took life from thee.
Mark but this flea, and mark in this,
How little that which thou deny'st me is;
It sucked me first, and now sucks thee,
And in this flea our two bloods mingled be;
Thou know'st that this cannot be said
A sin, nor shame, nor loss of maidenhead;
Yet this enjoys before it woo,
And pampered swells with one blood made of two,
And this, alas, is more than we would do.
Oh stay, three lives in one flea spare,
Where we almost, yea, more than married are.
This flea is you and I, and this
Our marriage bed, and marriage temple is;
Though parents grudge, and you, w'are met,
And cloistered in these living walls of jet.
Though use make you apt to kill me,
Let not to that, self-murder added be,
And sacrilege, three sins in killing three.

www.ingramcontent.com/pod-product-compliance
Lightning Source LLC
Chambersburg PA
CBHW040856100426
42813CB00015B/2812